'Their fru [D0795429]
diverse and
plentiful, as
nutmegs, ginger,
long pepper,
lemons,
cucumbers,
cocos, sago, with
divers other
sorts . . .'

RICHARD HAKLUYT
Born *c.* 1552, Hereford
Died 1616, London

HAKLUYT IN PENGUIN CLASSICS
Voyages and Discoveries

RICHARD HAKLUYT

The Voyage of Sir Francis Drake
Around the Whole Globe

PENGUIN BOOKS

PENGUIN CLASSICS

Published by the Penguin Group
Penguin Books Ltd, 80 Strand, London WC2R ORL, England
Penguin Group (USA) Inc., 375 Hudson Street, New York, New York 10014, USA
Penguin Group (Canada), 90 Eglinton Avenue East, Suite 700, Toronto, Ontario,
Canada M4P 2Y3 (a division of Pearson Penguin Canada Inc.)
Penguin Ireland, 25 St Stephen's Green, Dublin 2, Ireland
(a division of Penguin Books Ltd)
Penguin Group (Australia), 707 Collins Street, Melbourne, Victoria 3008, Australia
(a division of Pearson Australia Group Pty Ltd)
Penguin Books India Pvt Ltd, 11 Community Centre, Panchsheel Park,
New Delhi – 110 017, India
Penguin Group (NZ), 67 Apollo Drive, Rosedale, Auckland 0632, New Zealand
(a division of Pearson New Zealand Ltd)
Penguin Books (South Africa) (Pty) Ltd, Block D, Rosebank Office Park,
181 Jan Smuts Avenue, Parktown North, Gauteng 2193, South Africa

Penguin Books Ltd, Registered Offices: 80 Strand, London WC2R ORL, England

www.penguin.com

This selection published in Penguin Classics 2015
001

Set in 9/12.4 pt Baskerville 10 Pro
Typeset by Jouve (UK), Milton Keynes
Printed in Great Britain by Clays Ltd, St Ives plc

A CIP catalogue record for this book is available from the British Library

ISBN: 978-0-141-39851-8

www.greenpenguin.co.uk

Contents

The famous voyage of Sir Francis Drake into the South Sea, and there hence about the whole globe of the earth, begun in the year of our Lord, 1577.

The 15 day of November, in 1577, Mr Francis Drake, with a fleet of five ships and barks, and 164 men, gentlemen and sailors, departed from Plymouth, giving out his pretended voyage for Alexandria.

Upon the coast of Barbary, the 27 day we found an island called Mogador, between which island and the main, we found a very good and safe harbour for our ships to ride in.

On this island our general erected a pinnace, whereof he brought out of England with him four already framed.

We departed from this place the last day of December, and coasting along the shore, we did descry certain Spanish fishermen to whom we gave chase and took three of them, and proceeding further we met with three caravels and took them also.

The 17 day of January we arrived at Cabo Blanco, where we remained 4 days, and in that space our general mustered, and trained his men on land in warlike manner, to make them fit for all occasions.

We departed this harbour the 22 of January, carrying along with us one of the Portuguese caravels which was bound to the islands of Cape Verde for salt.

Upon one of those islands called Maio, we gave ourselves a little refreshing. The island is wonderfully stored with goats and wild hens, and it hath salt also without labour, the people gather it into heaps, which continually in great quantity is increased upon the sands by the flowing of the sea, and the receiving heat of the sun.

Amongst other things we found here a kind of fruit called cocos, which because it is not commonly known with us in England, I thought good to make some description of it.

The tree beareth no leaves nor branches, but at the very top the fruit groweth in clusters, hard at the top of the stem of the tree, as big every several fruit as a man's head: but having taken off the uttermost bark, which you shall find to be very full of strings or sinews, as I may term them, you shall come to a hard shell which may hold of quantity in liquor a pint commonly, or some a quart, and some less: within that shell of the thickness of half an inch good, you shall have a kind of hard substance and very white, no less good and sweet than almonds: within that again a certain clear liquor, which being drunk, you shall not only find it very delicate and sweet, but most comfortable and cordial.

Our general departed hence the 31 of this month, and sailed by the island of San Tiago, but far enough from the danger of the inhabitants, who shot and discharged at us three pieces, but they all fell short of us, and did us no harm. The mountains and high places of the island are said to be possessed by the Moors, who having been slaves to the Portuguese, made escape to the desert places of the island, where they abide with great strength.

We espied two ships under sail, to the one of which we

gave chase, and in the end boarded her with a ship-boat without resistance, and she yielded unto us good store of wine.

Being departed from these islands, we drew towards the line, where we were becalmed the space of 3 weeks, but yet subject to diverse great storms, terrible lightnings and much thunder: but with this misery we had the commodity of great store of fish, as dolphins, bonitos, and flying fishes, whereof some fell into our ships, where hence they could not rise again for want of moisture, for when their wings are dry, they cannot fly.

The first land that we fell with was the coast of Brazil, which we saw the fifth of April in the height of 33 degrees towards the pole Antarctic, and being discovered at sea by the inhabitants of the country, they made upon the coast great fires for a sacrifice (as we learned) to the devils, about which they use conjurations, making heaps of sand and other ceremonies, that when any ship shall go about to stay upon their coast, not only sands may be gathered together into shoals in every place, but also that storms and tempests may arise, to the casting away of ships and men.

The place where we met, our general called the Cape of Joy, where every ship took in some water. Here we found a good temperature and sweet air, a very fair and pleasant country with an exceedingly fruitful soil, where were great store of large and mighty deer, but we came not to the sight of any people: but travelling further into the country, we perceived the footing of people in the clay-ground, showing that they were men of great stature. Being returned to our ships, we weighed anchor, and harboured ourselves between a rock and the main, where by means of the rock that broke the force of the sea, we rode very safe, and upon this rock we killed for our provision certain sea-wolves, commonly called with us seals.

From hence we went our course to 36 degrees, and entered the great river of Plate, and ran into 54 and 55 fathoms and a half of fresh water, but our general finding here no good harbour, as he thought he should, bare out again to sea the 27 of April, but we sailing along, found a fair and reasonable good bay wherein were many, and the same profitable islands, one whereof had so many seals, as would at the least have laden all our ships.

Our general being on shore in an island, the people of the country showed themselves unto him, leaping and dancing, and entered into traffic with him, but they would not receive any things at any man's hands, but the same must be cast upon the ground. They are of clean, comely, and strong bodies, swift on foot, and seem to be very active.

We watered and made new provision of victuals, as by seals, whereof we slew to the number of 200 or 300 in the space of an hour.

The next day, we harboured ourselves again in a very good harbour, called by Magellan Puerto San Julián, where we found a gibbet standing upon the main, which we supposed to be the place where Magellan did execution upon some of his disobedient and rebellious company.

In this port our general began to enquire diligently of the actions of Mr Thomas Doughty, and found them not to be such as he looked for, but tending rather to contention or mutiny, whereby (without redress) the success of the voyage might greatly have been hazarded: whereupon the company was called together and made acquainted with the particulars of the cause, which were found partly by Master Doughty's own confession, and partly by the evidence of the fact, to be true: which when our general saw, although his private affection to Mr Doughty (as he then in the presence of us all sacredly protested) was great, yet the care he had of the state of the voyage, of the expectation of Her Majesty, and of the honour of his country did more touch him (as indeed it ought), than the private respect of one man: so that the cause being thoroughly heard, and all things done in good order as near as might be to the course of our laws in England, it was concluded that Mr Doughty should receive punishment according to the quality of the offence: he seeing no remedy but patience for himself, desired before his death to receive the communion, which he did at the hands of Mr Fletcher our minister, and our general himself accompanied him in that holy action: which being done, and the place of execution made ready, he having embraced our general and taken his leave of all the company, with prayer for the Queen's Majesty and our realm, in quiet sort laid his head to the block, where he ended his life. This being done, our general made divers speeches to the whole company, persuading us to unity, obedience, love, and regard of our voyage; and for the better confirmation thereof, willed every man the next Sunday following to prepare himself to receive the communion, as Christian brethren and friends ought to do, which was done in very reverent sort, and so with good contentment every man went about his business.

The 20 day we fell with the Strait of Magellan going into

the South Sea, at the cape or headland whereof we found the body of a dead man, whose flesh was clean consumed.

In this strait there be many fair harbours, with store of fresh water, but yet they lack their best commodity: for the water is there of such depth, that no man shall find ground to anchor in, except it be in some narrow river or corner, or between some rocks, so that if any extreme blasts or contrary winds do come (whereunto the place is much subject) it carrieth with it no small danger.

The land on both sides is very huge and mountainous, covered with snow. This strait is extremely cold, with frost and snow continually; the trees seem to stoop with the burden of the weather, and yet are green continually, and many good and sweet herbs do very plentifully grow and increase under them.

The 24 of August we arrived at an island in the straits, where we found great store of fowl which could not fly, of the bigness of geese, whereof we killed in less than one day 3,000 and victualled ourselves thoroughly therewith.

The seventh day we were driven by a great storm from the entering into the South Sea two hundred leagues and odd in longitude, and one degree to the southward of the Strait: in which height, and so many leagues to the westward, the fifteenth day of September fell out the eclipse of the moon at the hour of six of the clock at night: But neither did the ecliptical conflict of the moon impair our state, nor her clearing again amend us a whit, but the accustomed eclipse of the sea continued in his force, we being darkened more than the moon seven fold.

From the bay (which we called the Bay of Severing of

Friends) we were driven back to the southward of the straits in 57 degrees and a tierce: in which height we came to an anchor among the islands, having there fresh and very good water, with herbs of singular virtue. Not far from hence we entered another bay, where we found people both men and women in their canoes, naked, and ranging from one island to another to seek their meat, who entered traffic with us for such things as they had.

We returning hence northward again, found the 3 of October three islands, in one of which was such plenty of birds as is scant credible to report.

We ran, supposing the coast of Chile to lie as the general maps have described it, namely northwest, which we found to lie and trend to the northeast and eastwards, whereby it appeareth that this part of Chile hath not been truly hitherto discovered, or at least not truly reported for the space of 12 degrees at the least, being set down either of purpose to deceive, or of ignorant conjecture.

The 29 of November we cast anchor, and our general hoisting out our boat, went with ten of our company to shore, where we found people, whom the cruel and extreme dealings of the Spaniards have forced for their own safety and liberty to flee from the main, and to fortify themselves in this island. The people came down to us to the waterside with show of great courtesy, bringing to us potatoes, roots, and two very fat sheep, which our general received and gave them other things for them, and had promise to have water there: but the next day repairing again to the shore, and sending two men a land with barrels to fill water, the people taking them for Spaniards (to whom they use to show no favour if

7

they take them) laid violent hands on them, and as we think, slew them.

Our general seeing this, stayed here no longer, but weighed anchor, and set sail towards the coast of Chile, and drawing towards it, we met near to the shore an Indian in a canoe, who thinking us to have been Spaniards, came to us and told us, that at a place called Santiago, there was a great Spanish ship laden from the kingdom of Peru: for which good news our general gave him divers trifles, whereof he was glad, and went along with us and brought us to the place, which is called the port of Valparaíso.

We found indeed the ship riding at anchor, having in her eight Spaniards and three negroes, who thinking us to have been Spaniards and their friends, welcomed us with a drum: as soon as we were entered, one of our company called Thomas Moon began to lay about him, and struck one of the Spaniards, and said unto him, *abajo perro*, that is in English, go down dog. One of these Spaniards seeing persons of that quality in those seas, crossed and blessed himself: but to be short, we stowed them under hatches all save one Spaniard, who suddenly and desperately leapt overboard into the sea, and swam ashore to the town of Santiago, to give them warning.

They of the town being not above nine households, presently fled away and abandoned the town. Our general manned his boat, and the Spanish ship's boat, and went to the town, we rifled it, and came to a small chapel which we entered, and found therein a silver chalice, two cruets, and one altar-cloth, the spoil whereof our general gave to Mr Fletcher his minister.

We found also in this town a warehouse stored with wine of Chile, and many boards of cedar-wood, all which wine we brought away with us, and certain of the boards to burn for fire-wood: we departed the haven, having first set all the Spaniards on land, saving one John Griego a Greek born, whom our general carried with him for his pilot to bring him into the haven of Lima.

At sea, our general rifled the ship, and found in her good store of the wine of Chile, and 25,000 pesos of very pure and fine gold of Valdivia, amounting in value to 37,000 ducats of Spanish money, we arrived next at a place called Coquimbo, where our general sent 14 of his men on land to fetch water: but they were espied by the Spaniards, who came with 300 horsemen and 200 footmen, and slew one of our men with a piece, the rest came aboard in safety, and the Spaniards departed: we went ashore again, and buried our man, and the Spaniards came down again with a flag of truce, but we set sail and would not trust them.

From hence we went to a certain port called Tarapaca, where being landed, we found by the sea side a Spaniard lying asleep, who had lying by him 13 bars of silver, which weighed 4000 ducats Spanish; we took the silver, and left the man.

Not far from hence going on land for fresh water, we met with a Spaniard and an Indian boy driving 8 llamas or sheep of Peru which are as big as asses: every one of which sheep had on his back 2 bags of leather, each bag containing 50 lbs. weight of fine silver: so that bringing both the sheep and their burthen to the ships, we found in all the bags 800 weight of silver.

9

Here hence we sailed to a place called Arica, and being entered the port, we found there three small barks which we rifled, and found in one of them 57 wedges of silver, each of them weighing about 20 pound weight, and every of these wedges were of the fashion and bigness of a brickbat. Our general contented with the spoil of the ships, left the town and put off again to sea and set sail for Lima.

To Lima we came the 13 day of February, and being entered the haven, we found there about twelve sail of ships lying fast moored at an anchor; for the masters and merchants were here most secure, having never been assaulted by enemies. Our general rifled these ships, and found in one of them a chest full of royals of plate, and good store of silks and linen cloth. In which ship he had news of another ship called the *Cacafuego* which was gone towards Paita, and that the same ship was laded with treasure: whereupon we stayed no longer here, but cutting all the cables of the ships in the haven, we let them drive whither they would, either to sea or to the shore, and with all speed we followed the *Cacafuego*: but she was gone from thence towards Panama, whom our general still pursued, and by the way met with a bark laden with ropes and tackle for ships, which he boarded and searched, and found in her 80 lbs. weight of gold, and a crucifix of gold with goodly great emeralds set in it which he took, and some of the cordage also for his own ship.

We departed, still following the *Cacafuego*, and our general promised our company that whosoever could first descry her, should have his chain of gold for his good news. It fortuned that John Drake going up into the top, descried her about three of the clock, and about six of the clock we came to her and boarded her, and shot at her three pieces of ordnance, and struck down her mizzen, and being entered, we found in her great riches, as jewels and precious stones, thirteen chests full of royals of plate, fourscore pound weight of gold, and six and twenty ton of silver. The place where we took this prize, was called Cape de San Francisco, about 150 leagues from Panama.

We went on our course still towards the west, and not long after met with a ship laden with linen cloth and fine China-dishes of white earth, and great store of China-silks, of all which things we took as we listed.

The owner himself of this ship was in her, who was a Spanish gentleman, from whom our general took a falcon of gold, with a great emerald in the breast thereof, and the pilot of the ship he took also with him, and so cast the ship off.

This pilot brought us to the haven of Guatulco. We landed, and went presently to the town, and to the townhouse, where we found a judge sitting in judgement, being associate with three other officers, upon three negroes that had conspired the burning of the town: both which judges and prisoners we took, and brought them a shipboard, and caused the chief judge to write his letter to the town, to command all the townsmen to avoid that we might safely water there. Which being done, and they departed, we ransacked the town, and in one house we found a pot of the quantity of a bushel, full of reals of plate, which we brought to our ship.

And here one Thomas Moon one of our company, took a Spanish gentleman as he was flying out of the town, and searching him, he found a chain of gold about him, and other jewels, which he took, and so let him go.

Our general thinking himself both in respect of his private injuries received from the Spaniards, as also of their contempts and indignities offered to our country and prince in general, sufficiently satisfied and revenged: and supposing that Her Majesty at his return would rest content with this service, purposed to continue no longer upon the Spanish coasts, but began to consider and to consult the best way for his country.

He thought it not good to return by the Straits, for two special causes: the one, lest the Spaniards should there wait and attend for him in great strength, whose hands, he being left but one ship, could not possibly escape. The other cause was the dangerous situation of the mouth of the Straits in the South Sea, where continual storms blustering, as he found by experience, besides the shoals and sands upon the coast, he thought it not a good course to adventure that way: he resolved therefore to avoid these hazards, to go forward to the islands of the Moluccas, and there hence to sail the course of the Portuguese by the Cape of Buena Esperanza.

Upon this resolution, he began to think of his best way to the Moluccas, and finding himself where he now was becalmed, he saw that of necessity he must sail somewhat northerly to get a wind. We therefore set sail, and sailed 600 leagues at the least for a good wind.

The 5 day of June, being in 43 degrees towards the pole Arctic, we found the air so cold, that our men being grievously pinched with the same, complained of the extremity thereof, and the further we went, the more the cold increased upon us. Whereupon we thought it best for that time to seek the land, and did so, finding it not mountainous, but low plain land, till we came within 38 degrees, it pleased God to send us into a fair and good bay, with a good wind to enter the same.

In this bay we anchored, and the people of the country having their houses close by the water's side, showed themselves unto us, and sent a present to our general.

When they came unto us, they greatly wondered at the things that we brought, but our general (according to his natural and accustomed humanity) courteously entreated them, and liberally bestowed on them necessary things to cover their nakedness, whereupon they supposed us to be gods, and would not be persuaded to the contrary.

Their houses are digged round about with earth, and have clefts of wood set upon them, joining close together at the top like a spire steeple, which by reason of that closeness are very warm.

Their beds is the ground with rushes strewed on it, and lying about the house, have the fire in the midst. The men go naked, the women take bulrushes, and comb them after the manner of hemp, and thereof make their loose garments, which being knit about their middles, hang down about their hips, having also about their shoulders a skin of deer, with the hair upon it. These women are very obedient and serviceable to their husbands.

After they were departed from us, they came and visited us the second time, and brought with them feathers and bags of tobacco for presents: and when they came to the top of the hill (at the bottom whereof we had pitched our tents) they stayed themselves: where one appointed for speaker wearied himself with making a long oration, which done, they left their bows upon the hill, and came down with their presents.

In the meantime the women remaining on the hill, tormented themselves lamentably, tearing their flesh from their cheeks, whereby we perceived that they were about a sacrifice. In the meantime our general with his company went to prayer, and to reading of the Scriptures, at which exercise they were attentive, and seemed greatly to be affected with it.

The news of our being there spread through the country, the people that inhabited round about came down, and amongst them the king himself, a man of a goodly stature, and comely personage.

In the forefront was a man, who bore the sceptre or mace before the king, whereupon hanged two crowns, a lesser and a bigger, with three chains of a marvellous length: the crowns were made of knit work wrought artificially with feathers of divers colours: the chains were made of a bony substance, and few be the persons among them that are admitted to wear them. Next unto him, was the king himself, with his guard about his person, clad with coney skins, and other skins: after them followed the naked common sort of people, every one having his face painted, some with white, some with black, and other colours.

In the meantime our general gathered his men together, and marched within his fenced place, making against their approaching a very war-like show.

In coming towards our bulwarks and tents, the sceptre-bearer began a song observing his measures in a dance, and that with a stately countenance, whom the king with his guard, and every degree of persons following, did in like manner sing and dance, saving only the women, which danced and kept silence. The general permitted them to enter within our bulwark, where they continued their song and dance a reasonable time. They made signs to our general to sit down, to whom the king, and divers others made supplications, that he would take their province into his hand, and become their king, making signs that they would resign unto him their right and title of the whole land, and become his subjects. In which, to persuade us the better, the king and the rest, with one consent, and with great reverence, joyfully singing a song, did set the crown upon his head, enriched his neck with all their chains: which thing our general thought not meet to reject, because he knew not what honour and profit it might be to our country. Wherefore in the name, and to the use of Her Majesty he took the sceptre, crown, and dignity of the said country into his hands.

Our necessary business being ended, our general with his company travelled up into the country to their villages, where we found herds of deer by 1,000 in a company, being most large, and fat of body.

Our general called this country Nova Albion, and that for two causes: the one in respect of the white cliffs, which lie towards the sea: and the other, because it might have some affinity with our country in name, which sometime was so called.

There is no part of earth here to be taken up, wherein there is not some probable show of gold or silver.

At our departure hence our general set up a monument of our being there, as also of Her Majesty's right and title to the same, namely a plate, nailed upon a fair great post, whereupon was engraved Her Majesty's name, the day and year of our arrival there, with the free giving up of the province and people into Her Majesty's hands, together with Her Highness' picture and arms, in a piece of six pence of current English money under the plate, whereunder was also written the name of our general.

It seemeth that the Spaniards hitherto had never been in this part of the country, neither did ever discover the land by many degrees, to the southwards.

After we had set sail from hence, we continued without sight of land till the 13 day of October, which day we fell with certain islands 8 degrees to the northward of the line, from which came a great number of canoes, having in some of them 4 in some 6 and in some also 14 men, bringing with them cocos, and other fruits. Their canoes were hollow within, and cut with great art and cunning, being very smooth within and without, having a prow, and a stern of one sort, yielding inward circle-wise, being of a great height, and full of certain white shells for a bravery, and on each side of them lie out two pieces of timber about a yard and a half long, more or less.

This people have the nether part of their ears cut into a round circle, hanging down very low upon their cheeks, whereon they hang things of a reasonable weight. The nails of their hands are an inch long, their teeth are as black as pitch.

We continued our course by the islands of Tagulada, Zelon, and Zewarra, being friends to the Portuguese, the first whereof hath growing in it great store of cinnamon.

The 14 of November we fell with the islands of Molucca,

next morning early we came to anchor, at which time our general sent a messenger to the king with a velvet cloak for a present, and token of his coming to be in peace, and that he required nothing but traffic and exchange of merchandise, whereof he had good store.

The king was moved with great liking towards us, and sent to our general, that he should have what things he needed. In token whereof he sent to our general a signet, and within short time after came in his own person to our ship, to bring her into a better and safer road than she was in at present.

The king sent before 4 great and large canoes, in every one whereof were certain of his greatest, attired in white lawn of cloth of Calicut, having over their heads from the one end of the canoe to the other, a covering of thin perfumed mats, borne up with a frame made of reeds for the same use, under which every one did sit in his order according to his dignity, to keep him from the heat of the sun, divers of whom being of good age and gravity, did make an ancient and fatherly show. There were also divers young and comely men attired in white, as were the others: the rest were soldiers.

These canoes were furnished with war-like munition, every man for the most part having his sword and target, with his dagger, besides other weapons, as lances, calivers, darts, bows and arrows.

They rowed about us, one after another, and passing by, did their homage with great solemnity.

The king was a man of tall stature and seemed to be much delighted with the sound of our music, to whom as also to his nobility, our general gave presents.

At length the king craved leave of our general to depart,

promising the next day to come aboard, and in the meantime to send us such victuals, as were necessary for our provision: so that the same night we received of them meal, which they call sago, made of the tops of certain trees, tasting in the mouth like sour curds, but melteth like sugar, whereof they make certain cakes, which may be kept the space of ten years, and yet then good to be eaten. We had of them store of rice, hens, unperfect and liquid sugar, sugar canes, with store of cloves.

The king having promised to come aboard, brake his promise, but sent his brother to make his excuse, and to entreat our general to come on shore, offering himself pawn aboard for his safe return. Whereunto the general consented not, upon mislike conceived of the breach of his promise. But to satisfy him, our general sent certain of his gentlemen to the court.

The king at last came in guarded with 12 lances covered over with a rich canopy, with embossed gold. Our men rising to meet him, he graciously did welcome, and entertain them. He was attired after the manner of the country, but more sumptuously than the rest. From his waist down to the ground, was all cloth of gold, and the same very rich: his legs were bare, but on his feet were a pair of shoes made of Cordovan skin. In the attire of his head were finely wreathed hooped rings of gold, and about his neck he had a chain of perfect gold, the links whereof were great, and one fold double. On his fingers he had six very fair jewels, and sitting in his chair of estate, at his right hand stood a page with a fan in his hand, breathing and gathering the air to the king. The fan was in length two foot, and in breadth one foot, set with

8 sapphires, richly embroidered, and knit to a staff 3 foot in length, by which the page did hold, and move it.

This island is the chiefest of all the islands of Molucca. The king with his people are Moors in religion, observing certain new moons, with fasting: during which fasts, they neither eat nor drink in the day, but in the night.

Our general considering the great distance, and how far he was yet off from his country, thought it not best here to linger the time any longer, but weighing his anchors, set out, and sailed to a certain little island to the southwards of Celebes, where we graved our ship, and continued there in that and other businesses 26 days. This island is thoroughly grown with wood of a large and high growth, very straight and without boughs, save only in the head or top, whose leaves are not much differing from our broom in England. Amongst these trees night by night, through the whole land, did show themselves an infinite swarm of fiery worms flying in the air, whose bodies being no bigger than our common English flies, make such a show and light, as if every twig or tree had been a burning candle.

When we had ended our business here, we weighed, and set sail: but having at that time a bad wind, with much difficulty we recovered to the northward of the island of Celebes, where by reason of contrary winds, we were enforced to alter to the southward again, finding that course also to be very hard and dangerous for us, by reason of infinite shoals which lie off, and among the islands. Upon the 9 of January in the year 1579 we ran suddenly upon a rock, where we stuck fast from 8 of the clock at night till 4 of the clock in the afternoon the next day, being indeed out of all hope to escape the danger: but our general showed himself courageous, and of a good confidence in the mercy and protection of God: and we did our best endeavour to save ourselves, which it pleased God so to bless, that in the end we cleared ourselves most happily of the danger.

We lighted our ship upon the rocks of 3 ton of cloves, 8 pieces of ordnance, and certain meal and beans: and then the wind (as it were in a moment by the special grace of God) changing from the starboard to the larboard of the ship, we hoisted our sails, and the happy gale drove our ship off the rock into the sea again, to the no little comfort of all our hearts, for which we gave God such praise and thanks, as so great a benefit required.

The 8 of February following, we fell with the fruitful island of Barateve. The people of this island are comely in body and stature, and of a civil behaviour, just in dealing, and courteous to strangers. The men go naked, saving their heads and privities, every man having something or other hanging at their ears. The women are covered from the middle down to the foot, wearing a great number of bracelets upon their arms, being made some of bone, some of horn, and some of brass, the lightest whereof by our estimation weighed two ounces apiece.

With this people linen cloth is good merchandise, whereof they make rolls for their heads, and girdles to wear about them.

Their island is both rich and beautiful: rich in gold, silver, copper, and sulphur, wherein they seem skilful and expert.

Their fruits be diverse and plentiful, as nutmegs, ginger, long pepper, lemons, cucumbers, cocos, sago, with divers other sorts: since the time that we first set out of our own country of England, we happened on no place, wherein we found more comforts and better means of refreshing.

We set our course for Java, where arriving, we found great courtesy, and honourable entertainment. This island is governed by 5 kings, whom they call Rajah.

Of these five we had four a shipboard at once, and two or three often. They are wonderfully delighted in coloured clothes, as red and green: their upper parts of their bodies are naked save their heads, whereupon they wear a Turkish roll, as do the Moluccans: from the middle downward they wear a pintado of silk, trailing upon the ground, in colour as best they like.

They have an house in every village for their common assembly: every day they meet twice, men, women, and children, bringing with them such victuals as they think good, some fruits, some rice boiled, some hens roasted, some sago, having a table made 3 foot from the ground, whereon they set their meat, that every person sitting at the table may eat, one rejoicing in the company of another.

They boil their rice in an earthen pot, made in form of a sugar loaf being full of holes, as our pots which we water our gardens withal, and it is open at the great end, wherein they put their rice dry, without any moisture. In the meantime they have ready another great earthen pot, set fast in a furnace, boiling full of water, whereinto they put their pot with rice, by such measure, that they swelling become soft at the first, and by their swelling stopping the holes of the pot, admit no more water to enter, but the more they are boiled, the harder and more firm substance they become, so that in the end they are a firm and good bread, of the which with oil, butter, sugar, and other spices, they make diverse sorts of meats very pleasant of taste, and nourishing to nature.

The French pox is here very common to all, and they help themselves, sitting naked from ten to two in the sun, whereby the venomous humour is drawn out. Not long before our departure, they told us, that not far off there were such great ships as ours, wishing us to beware: upon this our captain would stay no longer.

From Java we sailed for the Cape of Good Hope, which was the first land we fell withal: neither did we touch with it, or any other land, until we came to Sierra Leone, upon the coast of Guinea: we ran hard aboard the Cape, finding the report of the Portuguese to be most false, who affirm, that it is the most dangerous cape of the world, never without intolerable storms and present dangers to travellers.

This cape is a most stately thing, and the fairest cape we saw in the whole circumference of the earth, and we passed by it the 18 of June.

From thence we continued our course to Sierra Leone, on the coast of Guinea, where we arrived the 22 of July, and found necessary provisions, great store of elephants, oysters upon trees of one kind, spawning and increasing infinitely.

We arrived in England the third of November 1580 being the third year of our departure.

The prosperous voyage of the worshipful Thomas Candish of Trimley in the County of Suffolk Esquire, into the South Sea, and from thence round about the circumference of the whole earth, begun in the year of our Lord 1586, and finished 1588.

We departed out of Plymouth on Thursday the 21 of July 1586 with 3 sails, to wit, the *Desire* a ship of 120 tons, the *Content* of 60 tons, and the *Hugh Gallant* a bark of 40 tons: in which small fleet were 123 persons and victuals sufficient for the space of two years, Thomas Candish being our general.

The first of August we came in sight of Fuerteventura, one of the isles of the Canaries, about ten of the clock in the morning.

The 25 day we fell with the point on the south side of Sierra Leone.

On Sunday the 28 the general sent some of his company on shore, and there they played and danced all the forenoon among the negroes.

On Monday morning being the 29 day, our general landed with 70 men or thereabout, and went up to their town, where we burnt 2 or 3 houses, and took what spoil we would, which was but little, but all the people fled: and in our retiring

23

aboard in a very little plain at their town's end they shot their arrows at us out of the woods, and hurt three or four of our men; their arrows were poisoned, but yet none of our men miscarried at that time, thanked be God. Their town is marvellous artificially builded with mud walls, and built round, with their yards paled in and kept very clean as well in their streets as in their houses. These negroes use good obedience to their king. There were in their town by estimation about one hundred houses.

The first of September there went many of our men on shore at the watering place, and did wash shirts very quietly all the day: and the second day they went again, and the negroes were in ambush round about the place: the negroes rushed out upon our men so suddenly, that in retiring to our boats, many of them were hurt: among whom one William Pickman a soldier was shot into the thigh, who plucking the arrow out, broke it, and left the head behind: the poison wrought so that night, that he was marvellously swollen, and all his belly and privy parts were as black as ink, and the next morning he died.

The last of October running west southwest about 24 leagues from Cape Frio in Brazil, we fell with a great mountain which had an high round knop on the top of it standing from it like a town, with two little islands from it.

The first of November we went in between the Ilha de São Sebastião and the mainland, and had our things on shore, and set up a forge, and had our cask on shore: our coopers made hoops, and so we remained there until the 23 day of the same month: in which time we fitted our things, built our pinnace, and filled our fresh water.

The 17 day of December in the afternoon we entered into an harbour, where there is a wonderful great store of seals, and another island of birds which are grey gulls. These seals are of a wonderful great bigness, huge, and monstrous of shape, and for the fore-part of their bodies cannot be compared to any thing better than to a lion: their head, and neck, and fore-parts of their bodies are full of rough hair: their feet are in manner of a fin, and in form like unto a man's hand: they breed and cast every month, giving their young milk, yet continually get they their living in the sea, and live altogether upon fish: their young are marvellous good meat, and being boiled or roasted, are hardly to be known from lamb or mutton. The old ones be of such bigness and force, that it is as much as 4 men are able to do to kill one of them with great cowlstaves: and he must be beaten down with striking on the head of him: for his body is of that bigness that four men could never kill him, but only on the head. For being shot through the body with an arquebus or a musket, yet he will go his way into the sea, and never care for it at the present.

This harbour is a very good place to trim ships in, and bring them on ground, and grave them in: for there ebbeth and floweth much water: therefore we graved and trimmed all our ships there.

The 24 of December being Christmas Eve, a man and a boy went into a very fair green valley at the foot of the mountains, where was a little pit or well which our men had digged and made some 2 or 3 days before to get fresh water: this man and boy came thither to wash their linen: there were a great store of Indians which were come down and found the man and boy in washing. These Indians being divided on each side of the rocks, shot at them with their arrows and hurt them both, but they fled presently, being about fifty or threescore, though our general followed them but with 16 or 20 men. The man's name which was hurt was John Garge, the boy's name was Lutch: the man was shot clean through the knee, the boy into the shoulder: either of them having very sore wounds. Their arrows are made of little canes, and their heads are of a flint stone, set into the cane very artificially: they seldom or never see any Christians: they are as wild as ever was a buck or any other wild beast: for we followed them, and they ran from us as it had been the wildest thing in the world. We took the measure of one of their feet, and it was 18 inches long. Their use is when any of them die, to bring him or them to the cliffs by the sea side, and upon the top of them they bury them, and in their graves are buried with them their bows and arrows, and all their jewels which they have in their lifetime, which are fine shells which they find by the sea side, which they cut and square after an artificial manner: and all is laid under their heads. The grave is made all with great stones of great length and bigness, being set all along full of the dead man's darts which he used when he was living. And they colour both their darts and their graves with a red colour which they use in colouring of themselves.

The 6 day [of January] we put in for the Straits.

The 7 day between the mouth of the Straits and the narrowest place thereof, we took a Spaniard whose name was Hernando, who was there with 23 Spaniards more, which were all that remained of four hundred, which were left there three years before in these Straits of Magellan, all the rest being dead with famine. And the same day we passed through the narrowest of the Straits.

The ninth day we departed from Penguin Island, and ran south southwest to King Philip's city which the Spaniards had built: which town or city had four forts, and every fort had in it one cast piece, which pieces were buried in the ground, the carriages were standing in their places unburied: we digged for them and had them all. They had contrived their city very well, and seated it in the best place of the Straits for wood and water: they had built up their churches by themselves: they had laws very severe among themselves, for they had erected a gibbet, whereon they had done execution upon some of their company. It seemed unto us that their whole living for a great space was altogether upon mussels and limpets: for there was not anything else to be had, except some deer which came out of the mountains down to the fresh rivers to drink. These Spaniards which were there, were only come to fortify the Straits, to the end that no other nation should have passage through into the South Sea saving only their own: but as it appeared, it was not God's will so to have it. For during the time that they were there, which was two years at the least, they could never have anything to grow or in any wise prosper. And on the other side the Indians oftentimes preyed upon them, until their victuals grew so short, that they died like dogs in their houses, and in their clothes, wherein we found them still at our coming, until that in the end the town being wonderfully tainted with the smell and the savour of the dead people, the rest which remained alive were driven to bury such things as they had there in their town either for provision or for furniture, and so to forsake the town, and to go along the sea side, and seek their victuals to preserve them from starving, taking nothing with them, but every man his arquebus (some were not able to carry them for weakness) and so lived for the space of a year and more with roots, leaves, and sometimes a fowl which they might kill with their piece. To conclude, they were determined to have travelled towards the river of Plate, only being left alive 23 persons, whereof two were women, which were the remainder of 4 hundred. In this place we watered and wooded well and quietly.

There was a fresh water river, where our general went up with the ship-boat about three miles, which river hath very good and pleasant ground about it, and it is low and champaign soil, and so we saw none other ground else in all the Straits but that was craggy rocks and monstrous high hills and mountains. In this river are great store of savages which we saw, and had conference with them: they were men eaters, and fed altogether upon raw flesh, and other filthy food: which people had preyed upon some of the Spaniards before spoken of. For they had gotten knives and pieces of rapiers to make darts of. They used all the means they could possibly to have allured us up farther into the river, of purpose to have betrayed us, which being espied by our general, he caused us to shoot at them with our arquebuses, whereby we killed many of them.

During this time, which was a full month, we fed almost altogether upon mussels and limpets, and birds, or such as we could get on shore, seeking every day for them, as the fowls of the air do, where they can find food, in continual rainy weather.

The 24 day of February we entered into the South Sea: the first of March a storm took us. This storm continued 3 or 4 days, and for that time we in the *Hugh Gallant* being separated from the other 2 ships looked every hour to sink, our bark was so leak, and ourselves so weakened with freeing it of water, that we slept not in three days and three nights.

The 15 of March in the morning the *Hugh Gallant* came in between the island of Santa Maria and the main where she met with the admiral and the *Content* which had rid at the island called La Mocha 2 days: at which place some of our men went on shore with the vice-admiral's boat, where the Indians fought with them with their bows and arrows, and were marvellous wary of their calivers. These Indians were enemies to the Spaniards, and belonged to a great place called Arauco, and took us for Spaniards, as afterwards we learned.

This place which is called Arauco is wonderfully rich, and full of gold mines, and yet it could not be subdued at any time by the Spaniards, but they always returned with the greatest loss of men. For these Indians are marvellous desperate and careless of their lives to live at their own liberty and freedom.

We weighed anchor, and ran under the west side of Santa Maria island, where we rode very well in six fathoms of water.

There came down to us certain Indians with two which were the principals of the island to welcome us on shore, thinking we had been Spaniards, for it is subdued by them: who brought us up to a place where the Spaniards had erected a church with crosses and altars in it. And there were about this church 2 or 3 store-houses, which were full of wheat and barley ready threshed. The wheat and barley was as fair, as clean, and every way as good as any we have in England. There were also cades full of potato roots, which were very good to eat, ready made up in the store-houses for the Spaniards against they should come for their tribute. This island also yieldeth many sorts of fruits, hogs, and hens. These Indians are held in such slavery by them, that they dare not eat a hen or an hog themselves. Thus we fitted our-selves here with corn as much as we would have, and as many hogs as we had salt to powder them withal, and great store of hens, with a number of bags of potato roots, and about 500 dried dogfishes, and Guinea wheat, which is called maize.

The fifteenth [of April, 1587] we came thwart of a place called Morro Moreno, an excellent harbour: here we went with our general on shore to the number of 30 men: and at our going on shore upon our landing, the Indians of the place came down from the rocks to meet with us, with fresh water and wood on their backs. They are in marvellous awe of the Spaniards, and very simple people, and live marvel-lously savagely: for they brought us to their bidings about two miles from the harbour, where we saw their women and lodging, which is nothing but the skin of some beast laid upon the ground: and over them instead of houses, is noth-ing but five or six sticks laid across, which stand upon two forks with sticks on the ground and a few boughs laid on it. Their diet is raw fish, which stinketh most vilely. And when any of them die, they bury their bows and arrows with them, with their canoe and all that they have: for we opened one of their graves, and saw the order of them. Their canoes or boats are marvellous artificially made of two skins like unto bladders, and are blown full at one end with quills: they have two of these bladders blown full, which are sewn together and made fast with a sinew of some wild beast; which when they are in the water swell, so that they are as tight as may be. They go to sea in these boats, and catch very much fish with them, and pay much of it for tribute unto the Spaniards: but they use it marvellous beastly.

The 27 day we took a small bark, which came from Santiago. In this bark was one George a Greek, a reasonable pilot for all the coast of Chile. There were also in the said bark one Fleming and three Spaniards: and they were all sworn and received the sacrament before they came to sea by three or four friars, that if we should chance to meet them, they should throw those letters over board: which (as we were giving them chase with our pinnace) before we could fetch them up, they had accordingly thrown away. Yet our general wrought so with them, that they did confess it: but he was fain to cause them to be tormented with their thumbs in a wrench, and to continue them at several times with extreme pain. Also he made the old Fleming believe that he would hang him; and the rope being about his neck he was pulled up a little from the hatches, and yet he would not confess, choosing rather to die, than he would be perjured. In the end it was confessed by one of the Spaniards, whereupon we burnt the bark, and carried the men with us.

The tenth day [of May] the *Hugh Gallant* in which bark I Francis Pretty was lost company with our admiral.

The 17 of May we met with our admiral again, and all the

rest of our fleet. They had taken two ships, the one laden with sugar, molasses, maize, Cordovan skins, montego de porco, many packs of pintados, many Indian coats, and some marmalade, and 1000 hens: and the other ship was laden with wheat meal, and boxes of marmalade. One of these ships which had the chief merchandise in it, was worth twenty thousand pounds, if it had been in England or in any other place of Christendom where we might have sold it. We filled all our ships with as much as we could bestow of these goods: the rest we burnt and the ships also; and set the men and women that were not killed on shore.

The 20 day in the morning we came into the road of Paita, and being at an anchor, our general landed with sixty or seventy men, skirmished with them of the town, and drove them all to flight to the top of the hill which is over the town. We found the quantity of 25 pounds weight in silver in pieces of eight reals, and abundance of household stuff and store-houses full of all kind of wares: but our general would not suffer any man to carry much cloth or apparel away, because they should not cloy themselves with burthens: for they were five men to one of us: and we had an English mile and a half to our ships. Thus we came down in safety to the town, which was very well builded, and marvellous clean kept in every street, with a town-house or guild hall in the midst, and had to the number of two hundred houses at the least in it. We set it on fire to the ground, and goods to the value of five or six thousand pounds: there was also a bark riding in the road which we set on fire and departed.

The 25 day of May we arrived at the island of Puna, where is a very good harbour, where we found a great ship of the burthen of 250 tons riding at an anchor with all her furniture, which was ready to be hauled on ground: for there is a special good place for that purpose. We sunk it, and went on shore where the lord of the island dwelt, who had a sumptuous house marvellous well contrived: and out of every chamber was framed a gallery with a stately prospect into the sea on one side, and into the island on the other side, with a marvellous great hall below, and a very great storehouse at the one end of the hall: the most part of the cables in the South Sea are made upon that island. This great cacique doth make all the Indians upon the island to work and to drudge for him: and he himself is an Indian born, but is married to a marvellous fair woman which is a Spaniard.

This Spanish woman his wife is honoured as a queen in the island, and never goeth on the ground upon her feet: but when her pleasure is to take the air, she is always carried in a shadow like unto an horse-litter upon four men's shoulders, with a veil or canopy over her for the sun or the wind, having her gentlewomen still attending about her with a great troop of the best men of the island with her. But both she and the lord of the island with all the Indians in the town were newly fled out of the island before we could get to an anchor, by reason we were becalmed before we could get in, and were gone over unto the mainland, having carried away with them to the sum of 100,000 crowns.

This island is very pleasant: but there are no mines of gold nor silver in it. There are at least 200 houses in the town about the cacique's palace, and as many in one or two towns more upon the island, which is almost as big as the Isle of Wight. There is planted on the one side of the cacique's house a fair garden, with all herbs growing in it, and at the lower end a well of fresh water, and round about it are trees set, whereon bombazine cotton groweth after this manner: the tops of the trees grow full of cods, out of which the cotton groweth, and in the cotton is a seed of the bigness of a pea, and in every cod there are seven or eight of these seeds: and if the cotton be not gathered when it is ripe, then these seeds fall from it, and spring again.

There are also in this garden fig trees which bear continually, also pompions, melons, cucumbers, radishes, rosemary and thyme, with many other herbs and fruits. At the other end of the house there is also another orchard, where grow oranges sweet and sour, lemons, pomegranates and limes, with divers other fruits.

There is very good pasture ground in this island; and withal many horses, oxen, bullocks, sheep very fat and fair, great store of goats which be very tame, and are used continually to be milked. They have moreover abundance of pigeons, turkeys, and ducks of a marvellous bigness.

There was also a very large and great church hard by the cacique's house, whither he caused all the Indians in the island to come and hear mass: for he himself was made a Christian when he was married to the Spanish woman before spoken of, and upon his conversion he caused the rest of his subjects to be christened. In this church was an high altar with a crucifix, and five bells hanging in the nether end thereof. We burnt the church and brought the bells away.

The second day of June in the morning, by and by after break of day, every one of the watch being gone abroad to seek to fetch in victuals, some one way, some another, upon the sudden there came down upon us an hundred Spanish soldiers with muskets and an ensign, which were landed on the other side of the island that night, and all the Indians of the island with them, every one with weapons. Thus being taken at advantage we had the worst: for our company was not past sixteen or twenty; whereof they had slain one or two before they were come to the houses: yet we skirmished with them an hour and a half: at the last being sore over-charged with multitudes, we were driven down from the hill to the water's side, and there kept them play a while, until in the end Zachary Saxie, who with his halberd had kept the way of the hill, and slain a couple of them, as he breathed himself being somewhat tired, had an honourable death and a short; for a shot struck him to the heart: who feeling himself mortally wounded cried to God for mercy, and fell down presently dead. But soon after the enemy was driven somewhat to retire from the bank's side to the green: and in the end our boat came and carried as many of our men away as could go in her, which was in hazard of sinking while they hastened into it: and one of our men whose name was Robert Maddocke was shot through the head with his own piece, being a snap-hance, as he was hasting into the boat. But four of us were left behind which the boat could not carry: to wit, myself Francis Pretty, Thomas Andrewes, Stephen Gunner, and Richard Rose: which had our shot ready and retired ourselves unto a cliff, until the boat came again, which was presently after they had carried the rest aboard. There were six and forty of the enemy's slain by us, whereof they had dragged some into bushes, and some into old houses, which we found afterwards. We lost twelve men.

The self same day, we went on shore again with seventy men, and had a fresh skirmish with the enemies, and drove them to retire, being an hundred Spaniards serving with muskets, and two hundred Indians with bows, arrows and darts. This done, we set fire on the town and burnt it to the ground, having in it to the number of three hundred houses: and shortly after made havoc of their fields, orchards and gardens, and burnt four great ships more which were in building on the stocks.

The fifth day of June we departed, and turned up for a place which is called Rio Dolce, where we watered: at which place also we sunk the *Hugh Gallant* for want of men, being a bark of forty tons.

The 27 in the morning by the break of day we came into the road of Aguatulco, where we found a bark of 50 tons, laden with cacaos and anil which they had there landed: and the men were all fled on shore. We landed there, and burnt their town, with the church and custom-house which was very fair and large: in which house were 600 bags of anil to dye cloth; every bag whereof was worth 40 crowns, and 400 bags of cacaos: every bag whereof is worth ten crowns. These cacaos go among them for meat and money. For 150 of them are in value one real of plate in ready payment. They are very like unto an almond, but are nothing so pleasant in taste: they eat them, and make drink of them. This the owner of the ship told us.

[The 8 we came to the road of Chaccalla.] Our general sent up Captain Havers with forty men of us before day, we went unto a place about two leagues up into the country in a most villainous desert path through the woods and wilderness:

and in the end we came to a place where we took three householders with their wives and children and some Indians, we bound them all and made them come to the sea side with us.

Our general made their wives to fetch us plantains, lemons, and oranges, pine-apples and other fruits whereof they had abundance, and so let their husbands depart.

The 4 of November the *Desire* and the *Content*, beating up and down upon the headland of California, between seven and 8 of the clock in the morning one of the company which was the trumpeter of the ship going up into the top espied a sail bearing in from the sea with the cape, whereupon he cried out with no small joy, a sail, a sail: we gave them chase some 3 or 4 hours, standing with our best advantage and working for the wind. In the afternoon we got up unto them, giving them the broadside with our great ordnance and a volley of small shot, and presently laid the ship aboard, whereof the King of Spain was owner, called the *Santa Anna* and thought to be 700 tons in burthen. As we were ready on their shipside to enter her, being not past 50 or 60 men at the uttermost, we perceived that the captain had made fights fore and after, and having not one man to be seen, stood close under their fights, with lances, javelins, rapiers, and targets, and an innumerable sort of great stones, which they threw overboard upon our heads being so many of them, they put us off the ship again, with the loss of 2 of our men which were slain, and with the hurting of 4 or 5. We new trimmed our sails, and gave them a fresh encounter with our great ordnance and also with our small shot, raking them through and through, to the killing and maiming of many of their men. Their captain still like a valiant man with his company stood very stoutly not yielding as yet: our general encouraging his men afresh with the whole noise of trumpets gave them the third encounter with our great ordnance. They being thus discomforted and spoiled, and their ship being in hazard of sinking by reason of the great shot, whereof some were under water, within 5 or 6 hours fight set out a flag of truce, desiring our general to save their lives and to take their goods, and that they would presently yield. Our general of his goodness promised them mercy, and willed them to strike their sails, and to hoist out their boat and to come aboard: one of their chief merchants came aboard unto our general: and falling down upon his knees, offered to have kissed our general's feet, and craved mercy. The general of his great humanity, promised their lives and good usage. The said pilot and captain presently certified the general what goods they had within board, to wit, an hundred and 22 thousand pesos of gold: with silks, satins, damasks, with musk and divers other merchandise, and great store of all manner of victuals with the choice of many conserves for to eat, and of sundry sorts of very good wines. On the 6 day of November following we went into an harbour which is called by the Spaniards, Puerto Seguro.

Here the whole company of the Spaniards, to the number of 190 persons were set on shore: where they had a fair river of fresh water, with great store of fresh fish, fowl and wood, and also many hares and coneys upon the mainland. Our general also gave them great store of victuals, of garbanzos, pease, and some wine. Also they had all the sails of their ship to make them tents on shore, with licence to take such store of planks as should be sufficients to make them a bark. Then we fell to hoisting in of our goods, sharing of the treasure, and allotting to every man his portion. In division whereof the eighth of this month, many of the company fell into a mutiny against our general, which nevertheless were after a sort pacified for the time.

Our general discharged the captain, with provision for his defence against the Indians, both of swords, targets, pieces, shot and powder to his great contentment: but before his departure, he took out of this great ship two young lads born in Japan, which could both write and read their own language. He took also with him out of their ship, 3 boys born in the isle of Manila, the one about 15, the other about 13, and the youngest about 9 years old. The third remaineth with the right honourable the Countess of Essex.

He took also from them a Spaniard, which was a very good pilot unto the islands of Ladrones, where the Spaniards do put in to water, sailing between Acapulco and the Philippines: in which isles of Ladrones, they find fresh water, plantains, and potato roots: howbeit the people be very rude and heathens. The 19 day of November about 3 of the clock in the afternoon, our general caused the King's ship to be set on fire, which having to the quantity of 500 tons of goods in her we saw burnt into the water, and then set sail joyfully homewards towards England with fair wind: we left the *Content* astern of us. Thinking she would have overtaken us, we lost her company and never saw her after. We were sailing unto the isles of Ladrones the rest of November, and all December, and so forth until the 3 of January 1588, with a fair wind for the space of 45 days: and we esteemed it to be between 17 and 18 hundred leagues. We were coming up within 2 leagues of the island, where we met with 60 or 70 sails of canoes full of savages, who came off to sea unto us, and brought with them in their boats plantains, cocos, potato roots, and fresh fish, which they had caught at sea, and held them up unto us for to exchange with us; we made fast little pieces of old iron upon small cords and fishing lines, and so veered the iron into their canoes, and they caught hold of them and took off the iron, and in exchange of it they would make fast unto the same line either a potato root, or a bundle of plantains, which we hauled in: and thus our company exchanged with them until they had satisfied themselves with as much as did content them: yet we could not be rid of them. For afterward they were so thick about the ship, that it stemmed and broke 1 or 2 of their canoes: but the men saved themselves being in every canoe 4, 6, or 8 persons all naked and excellent swimmers and divers. They are of a tawny colour and marvellous fat, and bigger ordinarily of stature than the most part of our men in England, wearing their hair long: their canoes were as artificially made as any that ever we had seen: considering they were made and contrived without any edge-tool. They are not above half a yard in breadth and in length some seven or eight yards, and their heads and sterns are both alike: their sail is made of mats of sedges, square or triangle wise: and they sail as well right against the wind, as before the wind: these savages followed us so long, that we could not be rid of them: until in the end our general commanded some half dozen arquebuses to be made ready; and himself struck one of them and the rest shot at them: but they were so nimble, that we could not discern whether they were killed or not, because they would fall back into the sea and prevent us by diving.

The 14 day of January, by the break of day we fell with a headland of the isles of the Philippines. Manila is well planted and inhabited with Spaniards to the number of six or seven hundred persons: which dwell in a town unwalled, which hath 3 or 4 small block houses, part made of wood, and part of stone being indeed of no great strength: they have one or two small galleys belong to the town. It is a very rich place of gold and many other commodities; and they have yearly traffic from Acapulco in Nueva España, and also 20 or 30 ships from China, which bring them many sorts of merchandise. They bring great store of gold with them, which they traffic and exchange for silver, and give weight for weight.

The fifteenth of January we fell with an island called Capul. Our ship was no sooner come to an anchor, but presently there came a canoe rowing aboard us, wherein was one of the chief caciques of the island, who supposing that we were Spaniards, brought us potato roots, and green cocos, in exchange whereof we gave his company pieces of linen to the quantity of a yard for four cocos, and as much linen for a basket of potato roots of a quart in quantity; which roots are very good meat, and excellent sweet either roasted or boiled.

This cacique's skin was carved and cut with sundry and many strokes and devices all over his body. Presently the people of the island came down with their cocos and potato roots, and brought with them hens and hogs. Thus we rode at anchor all day, doing nothing but buying roots, cocos, hens, hogs, refreshing ourselves marvellously well.

The same day at night being the fifteenth of January 1588, Nicholas Roderigo the Portuguese, whom we took out of the great *Santa Anna* at the cape of California, desired to speak with our general in secret: our general understood, and asked him what he had to say. The Portuguese made him this answer. That the Spaniard which was taken out of the great *Santa Anna* for a pilot, had written a letter, and secretly sealed it and locked it up in his chest, meaning to convey it by the inhabitants of this island to Manila, the contents whereof were: that there had been two English ships along the coast of Chile, Peru, [and] Nueva España, and that they had taken many ships and merchandise in them, and burnt divers towns, and spoiled all that ever they could come unto, and that they had taken the King's ship which came from Manila and all his treasure, with all the merchandise that was therein: and had set the people on shore. Therefore he willed them that they should make strong their bulwarks with their two galleys. He further signified, that we were riding at an island called Capul at the end of the island of Manila, being but one ship with small force in it: if they could use any means to surprise us being there at an anchor, they should dispatch it: for our force was but small, and our men but weak, and that the place where we rode was but 50 leagues from them. Our general called for him, and charged him with these things, which at the first he utterly denied: but in the end, the matter being made manifest, the next morning our general willed that he should be hanged.

The people of this island go almost all naked and are tawny of colour. The men wear only a strop about their waists, of some kind of linen of their own weaving, which is made of plantain leaves, and another strop coming from their back under their twists, which covers their privy parts, and is made fast to their girdles at their navels.

Every man and man-child among them hath a nail of tin thrust quite through the head of his privy part, being split in the lower end and rivetted, and on the head of the nail is as it were a crown: which is driven through their privities when they be young, and the place groweth up again, without any great pain to the child: and they take this nail out and in, as occasion serveth: and for the truth whereof we ourselves have taken one of these nails from a son of one of the kings which was of the age of 10 years, who did wear the same in his privy member.

This custom was granted at the request of the women of the country, who finding their men to be given to the foul sin of sodomy, desired some remedy against that mischief. Moreover all the males are circumcised, having the foreskin of their flesh cut away. These people wholly worship the devil, and often times have conference with him, which appeareth unto them in most ugly and monstrous shape.

On the 23 day of January, our general Mr Thomas Candish caused all the principals of this island, and of an hundred islands more, which he had made to pay tribute unto him (in hogs, hens, potatoes and cocos) to appear before him, and made himself and his company known unto them, that they were English men, and enemies to the Spaniards: and thereupon spread his ensign and sounded up the drums, which they much marvelled at: they promised both themselves and all the islands thereabout to aid him, whensoever he should come again to overcome the Spaniards. Also our general gave them, in token that we were enemies to the Spaniards, money back again for all their tribute which they had paid: which they took marvellous friendly, and rowed about our ship to show us pleasure: at the last our general caused a saker to be shot off, whereat they wondered, and with great contentment took their leaves of us.

On the 21 day of February, being Ash Wednesday Captain Havers died of a most fervent and pestilent ague, to the no small grief of our general, who caused two falcons and one saker to be shot off, who after he was shrouded in a sheet and a prayer said, was heaved overboard with great lamentation of us all. After his death myself with divers others in the ship fell marvellously sick, and so continued in very great pain for the space of three weeks or a month by reason of the extreme heat of the climate.

The first day of March having passed through the straits of Java, we came to an anchor under the southwest parts of Java: where we espied certain of the people fishing by the sea side. Our general taking into the ship-boat certain of his company, and a negro which could speak the tongue, made towards those fishers, which having espied our boat ran on shore into the wood for fear: but our general caused his negro to call unto them: presently one of them came out to the shore side and made answer. Our general by the negro enquired of him for fresh water, which they found, and caused the fisher to go to the king and to certify him of a ship that was come to have traffic for victuals, and for diamonds, pearls, or any other rich jewels that he had: for which he should have either gold or other merchandise in exchange.

Two or three canoes came from the town unto us with eggs, hens, fresh fish, oranges, and limes. Our general weighed anchor and stood in nearer for the town: and as we were under sail we met with one of the king's canoes coming toward us. In this canoe was the king's secretary, who had on his head a piece of dyed linen cloth folded up like a Turk's turban: he was all naked saving about his waist, his breast was carved with the broad arrow upon it: he went bare-footed: he had an interpreter with him, which was a mestizo, that is, half an Indian and half a Portuguese, who could speak very good Portuguese. This secretary signified unto our general that he had brought him an hog, hens, eggs, fresh fish, sugar-canes and wine: (which wine was as strong as any aquavitae, and as clear as any rock water). Our general used him singularly well, banqueted him most royally with the choice of many and sundry conserves, wines both sweet and other, and caused his musicians to make him music. This done our general told him that he and his company were Englishmen; and that we had been at China and had had traffic there with them, and that we were come thither to discover, and purposed to go to Malacca. The people of Java told our general that there were certain Portuguese in the island which lay there as factors continually to traffic with them, to buy negroes, cloves, pepper, sugar, and many other commodities. This secretary of the king with his interpreter lay one night aboard our ship. In the evening at the setting of the watch, our general commanded every man in the ship to provide his arquebus and his shot, and so with shooting off 40 or 50 small shot and one saker, himself set the watch with them. This was no small marvel unto these heathen people, who had not commonly seen any ship so furnished with men and ordnance.

After the break of day there came to the number of 9 or 10 of the king's canoes so deeply laden with victuals as they could swim with two great live oxen, half a score of wonderful great and fat hogs, a number of hens which were alive, drakes, geese, eggs, plantains, sugar canes, sugar in plates, cocos, sweet oranges and sour, limes, great store of wine and aquavitae, salt to season victuals withal, and almost all manner of victuals else. Among all the rest came two Portuguese of middle stature, and men of marvellous proper personage; they were each of them in a loose jerkin and hose, which came down from the waist to the ankle, because of the use of the country, and partly because it was Lent, and a time for doing of their penance: they had on each of them a very fair and a white lawn shirt, very decently, only their bare legs excepted. These Portuguese were no small joy unto our general and all the rest of our company: for we had not seen any Christian that was our friend of a year and a half before. Our general used and entreated them singularly well, with banquets and music: they told us that they were no less glad to see us, than we to see them, and enquired of the estate of their country, and what was become of Dom Antonio their King, and whether he be living or no: for the Spaniards had always brought them word that he was dead. Then our general satisfied them in every demand: assuring them, that their King was alive, and in England, and had honourable allowance of our Queen, and that there was war between Spain and England, and that we were come under the King of Portugal into the South Sea, and had warred upon the Spaniards there, and had fired, spoiled and sunk all the ships along the coast that we could meet withal, to the number of eighteen or twenty sails. With this report they were sufficiently satisfied.

On the other side they declared unto us the state of the island of Java. First the plentifulness and great choice and store of victuals of all sorts, and of all manner of fruits as before is set down: then the great and rich merchandise which are there to be had. The name of the king of that island was Raja Bolamboam, who was a man had in great majesty and fear among them. The common people may not bargain, sell or exchange any thing with any other nation without special licence from their king: and if any so do, it is present death for him. The king himself is a man of great years, and hath an hundred wives, his son hath fifty. The custom of the country is, that whensoever the king doth die, they take the body so dead and burn it and preserve the ashes, and within five days next after, the wives go together to a place appointed, and the chief of the women, hath a ball in her hand, and throweth it from her, and to the place where the ball resteth, thither they go all, and turn their faces to the eastward, and every one with a dagger in their hand, (which dagger they call a kris, and is as sharp as a razor) stab themselves to the heart, and falling grovelling on their faces so end their days. This thing is as true as it seemeth to any hearer to be strange.

The men of themselves be very politic and subtile, and

singularly valiant, and wonderfully at commandment and fear of their king. For example: if their king command them to undertake any exploit, be it never so dangerous or desperate, they dare not nor will refuse it, though they die every man in the execution of the same. For he will cut off the heads of every one of them which return alive without bringing of their purpose to pass: they never fear any death. If any of them feeleth himself hurt with lance or sword, he will willingly run himself upon the weapon quite through his body to procure his death more speedily, and in this desperate sort end his days, or overcome his enemy. Moreover, although the men be tawny of colour and go continually naked, yet their women be fair of complexion and go more apparelled.

They told us further, that if their King, Dom Antonio would come unto them, they would warrant him to have all the Moluccas at commandment, besides, China, and the isles of the Philippines, and that he might be assured to have all the Indians on his side that are in the country. The next day being the 16 of March we set sail towards the Cape of Good Hope, on the southernmost coast of Africa.

The rest of March and all the month of April we spent in traversing that mighty and vast sea, between the isle of Java and the main of Africa, observing the stars, the fowls, which are marks unto the seamen of fair weather, approaching lands or islands, the winds, the tempests, the rains and thunders, with the alterations of the tides and currents.

The 11 of May in the morning one of the company went into the top, and espied land. This cape is very easy to be known. For there are right over it three very high hills standing but a small way one off another, and the highest standeth in the midst and the ground is much lower by the seaside.

This cape of Buena Esperanza is set down and accompted for two thousand leagues from the island of Java in the Portuguese sea charts: but it is not so much almost by an hundred and fifty leagues, as we found by the running of our ship. We were in running of these eighteen hundred and fifty leagues just nine weeks.

The eighth day of June by break of day we fell in sight of the island of Saint Helena.

This island is very high land, and lieth in the main sea standing as it were in the midst of the sea between the main land of Africa, and the main of Brazil and the coast of Guinea.

The same day about two or three of the clock in the afternoon we went on shore, where we found a marvellous fair and pleasant valley, wherein divers handsome buildings and houses were set up, and especially one which was a church, which was tiled and whited on the outside very fair, and made with a porch, and within the church at the upper end was set an altar, whereon stood a very large table set in a frame having in it the picture of Our Saviour Christ upon the Cross and the image of Our Lady praying.

There are two houses adjoining to the church, which serve for kitchens to dress meat in: the coverings of the said houses are made flat, whereon is planted a very fair vine, and through both the said houses runneth a very good and wholesome stream of fresh water.

There is also right over against the said church a fair

causeway made up with stones reaching unto a valley by the seaside, in which valley is planted a garden, wherein grow great store of pompions and melons: and upon the said causeway is a frame erected whereon hang two bells wherewith they ring to mass; and hard unto it is a cross set up, which is squared, framed and made very artificially of free stone, whereon is carved in ciphers what time it was builded, which was in the year of our Lord 1571.

This valley is the fairest and largest low plot in all the island, and it is marvellous sweet and pleasant, and planted in every place either with fruit trees, or with herbs. There are fig trees, which bear fruit continually, and marvellous plentifully: for on every tree you shall have blossoms, green figs, and ripe figs, all at once: and it is so all the year long. There be also great store of lemon trees, orange trees, pomegranate trees, pomecitron trees, date trees, which bear fruit as the fig trees do, and are planted carefully and very artificially with very pleasant walks under and between them, and the said walks be overshadowed with the leaves of the trees: and in every void place is planted parsley, sorrel, basil, fennel, aniseed, mustard seed, radishes, and many special good herbs: and the fresh water brook runneth through divers places of this orchard, and may with very small pains be made to water any one tree in the valley.

This fresh water stream cometh from the tops of the mountains, and falleth from the cliff into the valley the height of a cable, and hath many arms out of it, which refresh the whole island, and almost every tree in it. The island is altogether high mountains and steep valleys, except it be in the tops of some hills, and down below in some of the valleys, where marvellous store of all these kind of fruits before spoken of do grow: there is greater store growing in the tops of the mountains than below in the valleys: but it is wonderful laboursome and also dangerous travelling up unto them and down again by reason of the height and steepness of the hills.

There is also upon this island great store of partridges, which are very tame, not making any great haste to fly away though one come very near them, but only to run away, and get up into the steep cliffs: we killed some of them with a fowling piece. They differ very much from our partridges which are in England both in bigness and also in colour. For they be within a little as big as an hen, and are of an ash colour, and live in coveys twelve, sixteen, and twenty together.

There are likewise no less store of pheasants in the island, which are also marvellous big and fat, surpassing those which are in our country in bigness.

There are in this island thousands of goats, which the Spaniards call cabritos, which are very wild: you shall see one or two hundred of them together: they will climb up the cliffs which are so steep that a man would think it a thing unpossible for any living thing to go here. We took and killed many of them for all their swiftness.

Here are in like manner great store of swine which be very wild and very fat, and of a marvellous bigness: they keep altogether upon the mountains, and will very seldom abide any man to come near them.

We found in the houses at our coming 3 slaves which were negroes, which told us that the East Indian fleet, which were in number 5 sails, the least whereof were in burthen of 8 or 900 tons, all laden with spices and Calicut cloth, with store of treasure and very rich stones and pearls, were gone from the said island of Saint Helena but 20 days before we came thither.

This island hath been found of a long time by the Portuguese, and hath been altogether planted by them, for their refreshing as they come from the East Indies.

The 20 day of June having taken in wood and water and refreshed ourselves with such things as we found there, and made clean our ship, we set sail about 8 of the clock in the night toward England.

The third of September we met with a Flemish hulk which came from Lisbon, and declared unto us the overthrowing of the Spanish fleet, to the singular rejoicing and comfort of us all.

The 9 of September, after a terrible tempest which carried away most part of our sails, by the merciful favour of the Almighty we recovered our long wished port of Plymouth in England, from whence we set forth at the beginning of our voyage.